Your Secret Door to Happy

Poems to Help You Stop Thinking and Live More

Uplifting Poetry By
Jon DeVries

Featuring:

Morningstar, Boy in the Mirror, Your Secret Door to Happy, Coast of Starlight Dreams and 45 more new original poems....

***Warning:** The views given in this book very much reflect the views of the poet, whether anyone likes that or not.*

Ordering Information:
For details, contact jonchristopherdevries@gmail.com
or website: curtainofozpublications.com

Print ISBN: 979-8-35096-961-0
eBook ISBN: 979-8-35096-962-7

Printed in the United States of America on SFI Certified paper.

First Edition

Contents

FOREWORD

There are a lot of rules in modern day living. Rules about business, rules about marriage, rules about taxes, rules about where to park, where you can go, where you can't go. Almost anything you can think of these days has rules. And, if you don't follow them, something bad can happen sometimes.

But – there is one magical place where there are NO rules. And that is IMAGINATION and POETRY. And that is what drew me to poetry – the chance to freely express my imagination, imagery, fantasy, creation, inspiration and inventiveness -without rules. Imagination and rules are like oil and water – they don't mix.

But, I do have one rule, that is my own, when writing poetry. I won't write a poem unless I feel it could help someone. Help that person to feel better, to realize something about life, to trigger their own imagination and creativity or just to take their attention off of all the rules for a while.

And I hope this book of poems does all that for you. And if it even blows your mind at some points, don't blame me.

Jon DeVries, 2024

INTRODUCTION

I am a 17 year old enthusiastic, ambitious dreamer disguised in a 72 year old body. I am a total American, though I love people of all countries and customs. I grew up in the American educational system and lived to tell the tale, which is quite a feat.

I spent some years as a musician, but I prefer to write poetry and put the melody into my words (if you find yourself reading one of the poems in this book and hear a tune along with it, I am responsible for that, lol).

You will find some underlying messages in this book after you have read through it. One of them of is that I wrote this book for you, personally, not as a generality to a mass of people. Another is that I think there is a great deal of hope ahead for all of us in the future and we have to help put that there with our own enthusiasm, ambition and optimism. For sure, I believe that you are only going to get out of life what you create for it yourself. And I believe that, as long as you keep going, the force that can stop you does not exist.

Life does have pain, it has its sorrow, it has joy, it has elation, it has boredom and it has moments that shock you out of your skin. Life is hot, it's fast, it's challenging and can drive you crazy. That is one reason why poetry was invented – to soften the blow of just living life. And that is how I try to use it.

Finally, as we are all together here on this planet of 8 billion people, I believe that the real power in life is to love people despite all they might do to you and just keep on loving them regardless of all that.

So – enjoy.

Jon DeVries, 2024

TITLE POEM

YOUR SECRET DOOR TO HAPPY

YOUR SECRET DOOR TO HAPPY

Your secret door to happy might be
Beneath the false bottom of your lunch box,
Or at the very ends of your fingertips,
Or through the window of that cute, blonde fox.

You squeeze through a Hobbitt-style hole,
Run up endless golden steps to cobalt sky.
Hold your breath and whisper "I am here",
Open your eyes and let out one big sigh.

Door creaks open, sunfire beams leak out,
You feel your body relaxing and unwinding.
Straitjacket of stress vanishes into vapor,
In the lap of an emerald meadow you are reclining.

People you used to hate are smiling and laughing,
All elated that you finally made it here.
The world is perfect in each and every way,
Gone is all sadness, bitterness and fear.

Happy is near, happy is far, happy is right beside you,
You hold the key to that blissful, waiting portal.
Your secret door waits patiently for your permission,
To open and deliver you happiness immortal.

ORIENTATION: This Book is About You

STOP THINKING

WHO ARE YOU?

QUESTIONS

MY UNIVERSE

STOP THINKING

Perfection is what we feel we cannot own,
We love so we can taste life up and down.
We fear a diary of blank, friendless pages,
We postpone death with every beloved found.

We endless travel to find peace and meaning,
To match our pulse to sky and surging sea.
To lay, fulfilled, in a breeze amongst flowers.
And gaze, awestruck, in the face of eternity,

When we stop thinking - we start to understand,
When we dream - we make life bow and obey.
Make passionate love like you'll be dead by day's end,
Breathe into every precious second a cosmic ballet.

QUESTIONS

What questions have you waited endlessly to be asked?
What answers have been delayed to you forever?
What love has eluded you, that you really deserved?
What kindness have you failed to give another?

How would the world look had you created it complete?
How much would you exchange for affection unending?
How light would be your heart with sorrow vanquished?
How do you walk the path so sweet and ascending?

Where have gone all the people you loved in yesteryear?
Where are you going and is it where you intended?
Where do you draw the line in accepting failures?
Where is the ecstasy so anticipated and splendid?

Who is the one that would save your whole existence?
Who was it that ended your too-short, exultant youth?
Whose pretty face emerges when you lay down to sleep?
Who do you see when mornings tell the naked truth?

When was the last time you knew unlimited beauty?
When are you going to lose the protective shell?
When did you injure someone you completely adored?
When are you finally going to open up and tell?

Why live out this life in sorrow, anxiety and loss?
Why not change your mind and seize the reins?
Why can't you have the life you've always yearned for?
Why not grab the chance to break the chains?

Far is the longed-for objective never worked on,
Near is the dream that reads your paradise maps.
Far is the love that does not include your commitment,
Near is the ecstasy of devotion, control and climax.

Never forget the power you hold and can display,
You can trust yourself when emotions overtake you.
Life needs your full participation and creativity,
The future is your canvas to embellish and imbue.

WHO ARE YOU?

You're not your name or current street address,
You're not your body or the size of your shoe,
You're not your phone or social security number
So, please tell me, if you would – who <u>are</u> you?

You're not stupid, worthless or irresponsible.
You're not your failings, fears or tailspins,
You are your dreams, goals and aspirations,
You are the spark that starts the fire within.

You are light pouring brightly from your eyes,
You're the aura that shines around your body,
You're anticipation and joy in your lover's smile,
You are courage and inspiration out to infinity.

You are history and now and future,
Countless lives and stories you've lived.
You are beauty and allure and elegance
You are poetry and song in divine gift.

You are the maker of all things incredible,
The painter of the wind and sea and stone.
Your skyscrapers and bridges form a gallery,
Of the greatest works ever to be shown.

You are gentle rain, but forceful as a warhead,
An expanding, rising, supercell thunderstorm,
A golden bird flying high in deep-blue heavens,
A magician giving life to things unformed.

You're a pure vessel of intensity and hope,
- But somehow you need to hide all that.
Afraid your powers might offend or trespass,
Better to be like everyone else and lie flat.

Rip off the chains - we know who you really are,
A spirit of the ages, a lover of mankind,
Mother to vast millennia of generations,
The best friend anyone could ever find.

YOUR UNIVERSE

When I close my eyes, I see the real universe,
Not the matrix I've been carefully trained to see.
Depth and perception all flow soft and freely,
All limits are surpassed, outward to infinity.

When I lay down, I feel the force within me,
To change the world and make it sane again.
Energy flows fill my space and consciousness,
Coursing through my veins like spirit champagne.

Never has the power seemed so perceptible,
My soulmate tiger rests peaceful next to me.
Peace and friendship is all that I am aiming,
Happy future children, as far as I can see.

Love, not guns, is the might that will protect us,
That will project us out, other galaxies to explore.
Where starlight ends and your universe begins,
Pain and past and hurt, gone forevermore.

PART I:
THE LAND
BEYOND DREAMS

SAIL TO IMAGINATION

SKY AND SEA AND BIRD

HOME PLANET

A HOPE FOR MAN

SAIL TO IMAGINATION

The value of any man is in his imagination,
To see a tree as a mighty vertical warlord,
A cloud as an archangel patrolling above,
A river as the lifespring to be happily explored.

The other side of the moon is his playground,
An easel and canvas - his ticket to eternity.
Colors swirling round like toys to be played with,
Effects include beauty, motion and pure absurdity.

His tools of work are sensation, games and love,
He admires all life as a parent does their child.
Gazing to the heavens for divine inspiration,
Looking for flowers and thoughts that grow wild.

His thirst is to see things no one else has seen,
To see through the curtain to a masted sailing ship.
To play a symphony amongst the stars and planets,
His kind heart reaching all men for companionship.

His passport to the universe is his willingness to see,
He grace all he touches with life, fun and beauty.
He predicts tomorrow with the stories he concocts,
The creation of the future - his one and only duty.

To a banker he's totally crazy but, then, so what?
Imagination is far senior to taxes and corporations,
The sky shimmers above, other worlds call to him,
He's limitless and free and sailing to imagination.

16

SKY AND SEA AND BIRD

No screamed threats or fearmongering lies,
Can be heard in lofty god-graced soaring summits.
Headlines spewing out their daily river of bile,
Know no ear or eye in waterfall's ecstatic plummets.

Kind breezes caress the gentle sloping shores,
War and pain come round again like foul weather,
Oceans preside o'er silent deepwater mansions,
And sky and sea and bird go on forever.

Continents of forested rich emerald, gifted to us all,
Heavens of color palettes no Old Master could equal,
Still argue we must and divide and conquer, bitter,
Here they go again, quoth the soaring seagulls.

Endless summer swaths of fertile meadows resplendent,
Hawks and larks, cardinals, pheasants and bluebirds flying,
Filling golden skies with trills, screes and whistles,
While bombs and guns and missiles their beauty belying.

In every single man is a heart that cherishes nature,
A soul that longs for high-flown godly endeavor,
A prayer that calls for the end of strife, war and longing,
Where sky and sea and bird go on forever.

HOME PLANET

His whole life he felt he did not belong here,
No space was his, crowded out of possessions.
Doors locked, fences chained, soul forfeited,
Suffering for many hidden, unknown transgressions.

He was welcome only in his house, and then barely,
All seaside sand was owned, shiny hotels restricted.
Pretty girls in movies a universe away, unknown,
Living by himself - a long, slow, cold crucifixion.

He had dreams of far-flung places he could not name,
They hung like apparitions over hard stone of existence.
Glimpses where love was high, lofty and universal,
Where sapphire suns washed all in pink luminescence.

He sensed he was not from Earth, and somehow....
He heard the lilt of an alien flowing tongue.
He closed his eyes and saw a beach and foothills,
Across the galaxy, with a song he once had sung.

He realized the only way to get to home universe,
Was to cure the fate of all beings trapped here.
Release them from their own cruel self-oblivion,
Liberate their souls, their true spirits to re-appear.

To lead the way out of all misery and failing,
Make a sane, freed world for all to inhabit.
Then work together in a new ascending reality,
Across the universe and back to true home planet.

A HOPE FOR MAN

It sparkled like a child's eyes following a circus clown,
It wept like a wife - homecoming soldier in her arms.
It rose like an orb on a morning not forgotten,
And danced as a mistress, with all her secret charms.

It flashed a speck of light on calm dappled currents,
Cut like a beam of heaven through a rainy afternoon.
Glistened like a drop of morning's golden dew,
And flowed down a river from the mountains of the moon.

It launched like a missile to the waiting azure heavens,
Fell like a leaf whose autumnal time was finally here.
Laughed full and deep with ethereal satisfaction,
Warmed by a fire during a winter dark and clear.

It rested on your windowsill and smiled, contented.
Chuckled at your timid, eager, longing sighs.
Walked up and took you by both trembling shoulders,
Gazed deep and straight into your expectant eyes:

---A real hope for Man---

PART II: HEROES AND ASSASSINS

BE

Be the Path,
Be the Journey.
Be the Arrival,
Be the Sunset.

Be the Future,
Be the Past.
Be the Maybe,
Be the Truth.

Be the Victor,
Be the Vanquished.
Be the Storm,
Be the Silence.

Be the Lustful
Be the Pure,
Be the Wicked,
Be the Virgin.

Be the Maiden,
Be the General.
Be the Prophet,
Be the Vision.

Be the Surf,
Be the Shore.
Be the Wind,
Be the Waiting.

Be the Wheel,
Be the Stone.
Be the Fire,
Be the Ashes.

Be the Spirit,
Be the Shadow.
Be the Mountain,
Be the Meadow.

Be the Air,
Be the Arrow.
Be the Bullet,
Be the Wounded.

Be the Door,
Be the Fence,
Be the Key,
Be the Jailer.

Be the Honored,
Be the Damned,
Be the Priest,
Be the Gypsy.

Be the Option,
Be the Decision,
Be the Question,
Be the Answer.

Heroes and Assassins

Wind flurries
Night falls
Time beats its rhythm
Stones break bones

Sticks cover trees
Words never hurt me
Naked people want
What life won't give

Clothes hang drying
Desires to keep unseen
Extra Virgin oil lubes
Dreams vivid and close

Hammers shatter bricks
Hidden clues to reveal
Nightmares awake linger
Shredding night and day

Streetlights shelter nothing
Darkness all around
Love chapters our lives
With heroes and assassins

Counting on affection
Romantic windows closing
Kill the unforgiving soul
Caress the one that's loyal

Let the tide rise and ebb
Each climax to emblazon
Forget the losses
Remember little victories

Kiss the blazing sun
That scorches expectations
Enemies and companions
Idiots and savants

Rage and unbridled ecstasy
Heroes and Assassins

BEHIND THE FACADE

I am
I exist
I walk the streets
I follow the path
I follow the river to the source
I bend but do not break
The earth senses my steps
The moon shines on my adventures
Trees watch closely as I go by
Slow to answer.
Streetlights pass like naked ships
On seas of asphalt and sidewalk
Broken twigs like broken people
Severed promises line the shelves
Of stores out of business
To have a purpose is to be king
To have love is to be transported
Weather comes and goes, uncaring
Dumping on anyone who will listen
Shoes walk, but feet resist the outcome
Birds flee every tree they sit on
Clouds cannot be relied on to stay
Worn benches greet the losers
Of games ground into powder
Fire lights the faces of the lonely
Darkness covers secrets unforgotten

Streets link us all here together
Valleys hide what mountains cannot
Life pushes, pushes, pushes
Through cracks in the sidewalk
Overgrowing all it encounters
Uterus follows the blueprint
Another player to usher in

LANDFILL INMATES

Dice, rats, railroad ties, marbles,
porch swing, hammer, dust,
chains, lies, kitchen table,
masks, drums, porcelain rings.

Tree stumps, welcome mats, fire,
shards, drapes, bathtub gin,
spokes, blinds, eviction papers,
frames, flashlights, secrets.

Gutters, grandmas, Lucky Strikes,
hub caps, french fries, pliers,
ballerinas, snow chains, lime pie,
tubes, truck tires, lingerie.

Skinny dip, divorce, rain pants,
earrings, fenders, black cats,
rebar, butterflies, abortion tools,
leaky pens, condoms, pastor prayers.

Garage doors, gossip, brassieres,
spaghetti, driftwood, mirrors,
blindspots, ex-virgins, semi- trucks,
uncles, scandals, barbecue tongs.

Nylons, James Dean, poker bets,
rape, checkmate, shovel marks,
roosters, dreamsicles, Popeye,
lamps, turnpike, back seats, ashtray.

Trumpet, ice pick, avalanche,
infant, manuscript, coffin nails,
wineglass, mechanic, tornadoes,
hard-on, boardroom, pocket change.

Prom queens, barnyards, apple trees,
liquor, pain, dementia, algebra,
ice storm, masturbation, sunrises,
closet doors, altar bells, hot tubs.

Hymen, Maytag, whispers, light bulbs,
mortgages, moth balls, toasters,
rifles, roast beef, convertible tops,
breast pumps, time travel, hula hoops.

Sewer pipes, Sunday school, airline tickets,
Prozac, popcorn, penis envy, scholars,
library cards, libido, John Deere parts,
Big Pharma, Big Brother, cemetery.

Swat team, silk blouse, oven, creamery,
window ledge, American dream, cocaine,
grammar, erectile dysfunction, Cocoa Puffs,
barstools, golden rules, bikini bottoms.

Sympathy, superglue, campfire ashes,
Liquid Nails, pacemakers, undecided voters,
oil pans, Thanskgiving, diabetic socks,
infidelity, chocolate cake, wedding dresses.

THE FUTURE

It's the pent-up desire in a new lover's eyes,
The sparks flying off of a sun-spangled river.
The ethereal trill of a flight of golden sparrows,
The heartfelt pledge you hunger to deliver.

It's the pregnant woman walking proudly past,
The solemn promise made over burning fire.
The melody in your head you can't sing or place,
The silver songbird flying higher and higher.

It's the chain you link and the lock you set free,
The dark tunnel of mystery - wink of light ahead.
The note in the tossed-ashore last hope bottle,
The seed of the tree, the sacred vow yet unsaid.

It's the holy trinity of past, present and prophet,
The soul that listens and the spirit that deifies,
The girl you knew and the one around the corner,
The war that never started, the deep peace in her eyes.

It's a firestorm of passion, the stillness of true love,
The trail not discovered, the new star in the sky.
The brush that caresses the canvas - soft, kind and sure,
The poet entreating the cosmos and God's gentle reply.

The future is the reason why we're all still here.
The past couldn't hold us and the present is just now.
Busy building cathedrals and rigid steel skywalks,
To climb to our dreams and the ecstasies they endow.

PART III:
THREE DAYS SAIL
TO THE HEART

MY FUTURE LOVER

MORNINGSTAR

I WILL REMEMBER YOU

VENICE FOREVER

LOVE IS EVERYWHERE

LOVE RESPONSIBLY

UTOPIA FIRE

A MOST ILLOGICAL FRIDAY

TEN MILLION LOVERS

MY FUTURE LOVER

She is tall and thin and likes playing Scrabble,
Late at night, no clothes on – winner-take-all.
She drinks chocolate milk like it's a pink daiquiri,
Pleasant summer evenings is all she can recall.

She steps out of the shower wet, like Cleopatra,
Calling for her towel and nubile slave assistant.
The water clings to her in jealous beaded drops,
She's royal and cocky – close, but, oh, so distant.

She wears my shirts as if I never owned them,
Commandeers the bed - nary an "excuse me".
She says "no" and means "yes, please right now",
She's a land mine ready to go off inside me.

She's more gorgeous than a sky-wide meteor shower,
But loyal as a pitbull in a full-fledged fight.
She has a mythological grace and demeanor,
But washes down her pizza with warm Bud Light.

Think Barbie. Think Janis Joplin. Think Aphrodite.
You got the idea, she's one hell of a lady.
She plays a mean sax, loves the whole night long,
Wakes up and says, "You really drive me crazy."

My lover of the future is somewhere on a street,
Walking toward our collision, confident and pretty.
Faces move past me, not that one, maybe she?
As each sun rises, I feel her arrival, soft and free.

MORNING STAR

There is no peace like the quietude after
The sweat of a woman has covered you.

Her relaxed and satiated exhale against your ear,
The gradual diminishing of the trembling in her hips,
The low laugh that says "You had me".
The security of knowing you fully belong to each other.

Just two bare minutes ago, hearts pounding,
Fingers and toes curling and uncurling,
Her long, lithe legs over your shoulders,
Climbing you to the stars.

Planets and suns colliding, cosmic reverberation,
Souls penetrating souls to completion.

A morning star shines on the entwined, sleeping bodies.

I WILL REMEMBER YOU

I searched high and low for things I could take with me,
Past my demise, over the threshold, through the final curtain.
Into the new space, the next journey, when departed,
I started a list of all the things I would want there.

I could take my social security card – it's a legal document.
I could take my name – but, damn, I would forget it.
I could take my money – but where to pick it up??
I could take my clothes – no, they're stuck in the coffin!!

Okay, hold on, let's not panic or give up on this.
I could take my reputation – but who would know me?
I could take deed to my house – but there's a new owner!
I wept at the solidity of the barrier from here to there.

But --- if you came to me there with a smile I had not seen,
With a song I had not heard, I would still know you.
Even if decades were between us, I would know your aura,
Your gentle persona, the exhale of your spiraling essence.

Across the bridge, from here to there, we give up all things,
But love and life we keep and kiss of passion still burning.
Of bond and promise and summer days spent laughing,
Only this – the ultimate possession – only this.

VENICE FOREVER

Blood-red skies, crimson roofs, fire-orange canals,
Boats gliding silken waterways these 1800 years.
2 millenia of fiances vowing full faith forever,
Solemn promises ending in love forever or tears.

Gondoliers plying their trade, sunup to sundown,
Floating 10 feet above the city's tree trunk solid base,
A city of love and mystery, transcendent art,
Timeless lagoon watching, patient its eternal face.

Cross Ponte Rialto, a bridge of magic and history,
Where time stood still in the face of wars and strife.
Five bells of Saint Mark's ring out passing day and weeks,
Baptisms at Basilico Di San Marco, welcoming new life.

Island gondolas sliding waters where stood a powerful navy.
The birthplace of the galleon warship that sailed the world.
Now, peace and tranquility fills this Adriatic water paradise,
And a magic seaside sky every day created/unfurled.

City of art galleries, bursting with creative best of ages,
The frescoes of Ca'Rezzonico still brilliant, flaming colors,
Our water taxi driver smiles, understanding awe and wonder,
Proud to be part of the city and to live and love above her.

LOVE IS EVERYWHERE

Hate is stuck, drying concrete – heavy, dark and dead,
Anger is stopped motion, stopped time - punch, slap, snuff.
Rage is cutting, slashing, bleeding streets to nowhere,
Arrogance is lonely, degrading, self-destroying stuff.

Love is soft brush on canvas, song in the wind, sighing,
It's admiration – dissolving, flowing, together, creating.
It's tenderness - a shoulder, a cheek, a hand, a thigh,
Intimacy - breathing, exhaling, flying, cascading.

Love is everywhere – unlock your mind and look.
Sparkling eyes, caressing words, exhilarated givings.
Love is everywhere – now create it all around you.
It's what you do best and it's why you are living.

LOVE RESPONSIBLY

Just realize that when you see a beautiful woman
And your temperature rises, and she looks back at you,
And her temperature rises,

That there is a symphony orchestra waiting behind
the curtains and the curtains are your clothes,
And the violins are her legs and the kettle drums
are your hips,

And the crescendoes that follow are life in its
never-ending push to eternity and beyond.

So -------- love responsibly...

COAST OF STARLIGHT DREAMS

Dawn's light breaks on the far side of the moon,
Spring buds bursting through winter's lonely tomb.
Clear voices ringing out in dark and gloomy night,
Children running at me with faces clean and bright.

Cool emerald water bathing limbs and drifting by,
Soft white pillow clouds perched high up in the sky.
Birds soaring through it all, racing fast and proud,
Seeing home at long last and laughing right out loud.

Summer nights floating down the coast of starlight dreams,
Running fast to find the place where all is as it seems.
Where love is love and hope is hope and time everlasting,
And everything I ever wanted is all that I am asking.

Sleep my love and carry me to moonlight heaven meadows,
Live with me past city limits, past dark, lonely shadows.
Touch me and take me where our passion light shines,
And by the light of God's own sun, be my Valentine.

UTOPIA FIRE

Infinity is depth of emerald shining eyes.
Eternity is buttons resisting slow, one by one,
Limitless is passion in just one ragged breath,
Endlessness is inside her soft heavenly space.

Raven hair spills down soft, silken shoulders.
Her back an island for ones lost at spiritual sea.
Her arms encircling my universe longingly fastened,
Skin of hot burning fiery utopia long breaths.

How the sun shines is a very simple question,
How the moon glows is known in hidden places.
Where her heart is - divinity's jurisdiction only,
Where her hands are - impossible to predict.

Clocks guard time, but there is no time here,
Minutes take hours, days flash into seconds.
Kaleidoscopes multiply and saturate space,
Face of God appears and fades into conception.

A MOST ILLOGICAL FRIDAY

It was a gusty, stormy late Friday evening,
She was late to the bus, a soaked white Cinderella.
The rain fell in torrents as we ran past each other.
I tripped on her dress, she fell over my umbrella,

She was high society, I drove an old beer truck,
Different universes come flying hard together.
Her accent regal, mine lowly South Boston,
But there was something going on more than weather.

"Sorry", I said, as I untangled from her accessories,
The rain coming down like Fury herself descending.
She sat on the ground, awaiting noble rescue,
I looked all around – it was only me attending.

"Hurt yourself?" I said, trying to appear concerned,
But lost in her face I only seen in a magazine.
"We don't even know each other", she said abruptly,
"Pick me up right now, before I start to scream".

She was light as a feather, all dress and bra and things,
"Watch where you put your big hands", she dictated.
Helped her to her feet – I figured we were finished,
But she put her hand on my shoulder and just waited.

I wasn't much for looking right direct at ladies,
But mustered up a smile despite my timid doubt.
"You live around here?" she murmured *intently*,
And walked beside me like we was goin out.

"Up by the river, down the lower side", I said,
"But not that far, if we can get there without drownin",
"Let's make it fast" she said and pulled on my arm,
"I can't be seen here with you ---- and stop frowning!"

We got to my door, up the stairs and fell inside,
Soaked to the skin, I lit the fire and held a chair.
She looked at me closely, took a seat and shed her hat,
The sheer unlikelihood of this whole, rainy affair!

She asked to dry her clothes, was there such a place?
I felt a little dizzy, motioned a nook by the fire.
She took off her shawl and dress, flopped in a chair,
I tried not to gawp, but my eyes filled with desire.

She was a sight a poor man's eyes never to behold,
Like the gardener who catches the queen in bathing.
Skin of smooth golden hue that never held a tool,
Hair shimmering, shining and generally misbehaving.

She seemed to be chewing something over in her mind,
Then restlessness appeared with a deep, dark dismay.
I sat, held my tongue and watched her from afar,
Some picture in front of her that was not going away.

"I'm caged in my pretty little world", she finally said,
"Suffocating in conventions and infertile, tepid men.
You look strong and real and a working man by trade,
Do you have a wife or girl or someone you fancy, then?"

I gulped, fought for time, my mind did not work quickly,
She stared at me like a widow at a rich suitor's dance.
"I got no one really, I kind of keep to myself and drive,
But I had a girl once and wouldn't turn down the chance."

I was sure I'd seen the last of her, but sat there still she did,
Pensive look on her face and the kindness it implied.
She swung to her feet, swept the hair back off her neck,
I felt that motion in my soul and decided I would try.

"You seem so tender, like a mother with her babies,
But stormy as that north shore wind when she blusters".
She warmed her hands on the hot, glowing fire,
I summoned every ounce of courage I could muster.

"I'm not a rich man, I said, "but am straight and sincere,
I drive truck and my life is not interesting, it's true,
But I have passion for life and love that beats within me,
Our worlds are far apart, but I wish I could enfold you."

"We tripped and fell before", she said, "why not repeat?"
Pulled me to the floor, laughing softly in my ear.
"You're so very strong, you smell like a real live man",
Couldn't really believe that she was actually here.

With one hand, I held her clean up over my head,
She, giggling away all the feeble and sterile men.
Close to my chest, we rode all around the world,
In my best English – "would madam care for that again?"

The night carried on, all our clothes got good and dry,
The fire spat, sparkled and the gap between us died.
The beer truck laughed when I showed up Monday late,
A grin on my face, a new bounce I could not deny.

TEN MILLION LOVERS

I realized I must have had 10 million lovers.
How do you apologize to 10 million lovers?
How do you embrace 10 million lovers?
No one's arms are quite that big.

Each one of them a special being,
Each one of them a beautiful spirit,
Wars and births and deaths intervened,
But I never stopped loving any of them.

Where do 10 million lovers all go?
How could I possibly lose that many?
Surely, one or two of them would return,
Perhaps my teacher, my nurse, my wife?

Hiding behind their modern-day identity,
My 10 million lovers disguise themselves well,
But I feel it, when certain of them walk by,
Like a song I sang a very long time ago.

Do they ever think of me and wonder?
What town or city or home I live in now?
Do they wonder if I still harbor that love?
And gaze at night to the moon's low sigh?

Some say erase them, forget about the past,
But, somehow, they are in the future, too,
What goes around, comes around they say,
10 million lovers, forever through time.

PART IV:
IF YOU CAN
LAUGH

LORD KETO

It was a religious, rigorous discipline I assumed,
When the Lord Keto crossed my threshold.
One meal per day, no snacks allowed ever,
Sacred Kale and Celery and Spinach, behold.

Intermittent Fasting always done facing Mecca,
Reading food labels under an electron-microscope.
Fearing the grip of the dreaded soy and GMO,
And the FDA - here in the land of no food hope.

Shopping with my wife causing high marital stress,
"Jelly donuts are on sale!" leading to full-scale conflict,
"Only 40 grams of carbs!" violating nuptial contracts,
Try getting through checkout without an anxiety fit.

But I was ready for the next step, feeling pretty cocky,
"Do a week-long fast" was a mantra I could embrace,
Shunning all but tea, water and wheatgrass superfood,
Day 1, 2, 3 and 4, I was in a very good place.

Day 5 and 6, hallucinations of buffets 10 feet high,
And syrup running in the streets and carbohydrate binges.
Day 7, I felt a deep savage instinct snap in play,
And ripped the refrigerator door off its hinges.

Climax after climax, wolfing down Oreo cookies,
Spine-tingling joy of dripping Big Mac and Fries,
Velveeta bricks and plates of Twinkie/Pop Tarts,
I was off the chain, with all that that implies.

"He was such a fine young man", the mourners said,
"It's a mystery the Good Lord took him so early".
But I know what happened- why I left this Earth,
It was the dozen deep-fried, pancake-syrup-drizzled,
ham and cheese Krispy Cream jelly donuts.

Simply put --- they were to die for.

Inside Out

Girl Walks by Me:

To Her:

Good morning, how are you?
Well, I am fine. How are you?
Oh I am good. Nice day, yes?
Yes, it certainly is.

Inside:

Jesus, what a fox! Those legs are perfect!
God, what do I say to her?..............
Wow, those boobs shake when she walks!
Christ, another one got away. .....

Another girl is looking around, confused:

To Her:

Do you know where you are going?
I am not sure, does the bus stop here?
Yes, it does, right at noon.
You are so helpful, thank you.

Inside:

This IS the one – those emerald eyes!
Does she like me? Am I a just a dick?
I am so obviously staring at her!
Damn, another one got away....

My girlfriend walks up to me:

To Her:

Hi, how are you, honey?
Well, I still feel hung over from last night,
Yeah, that was a crazy night.
You're checking out the other girls, right? (she smiles)

Inside:

Wow, did she see me salivating over that chick?!
She isn't as hot as that girl I SHOULD have.
Oh god, she knows I am looking around,
Is she gaining weight, or is it my imagination?

..Whatever I do, I can't let the inside out!..

STRESS IS

Trying to love Man, despite the very dumb things he does.
Trying to create into the future with all your attention on the past.
Single-paper-bagging watermelons and making it to your car.
Realizing the guy honking angrily behind you is Highway Patrol.
Being asked to speak in front of the whole PTA meeting.
Flirting hard at a girl - then realizing she's your new boss.
Proposing to your fiance – grandmothers taking notes.
The hour's drive back to the store because you left your wallet.
Wondering if the guy you love is even paying attention.
Praying to God for help and getting a busy signal.
Watching your precious little children bungee jumping.
Eagerly picking your nose and the elevator door opens.
An erection while a hot female nurse shaves you for hernia surgery.
Trying to lose weight for your 40 year high school reunion.
Halfway to work and realizing your bra is on backwards.
Talking loudly in your sleep ----- to your old boyfriends.
Realizing you are going to pass major gas at Easter Service.
Falling asleep after you put 24 eggs onto high boil.
Your old girlfriend introducing a son you didn't know she had....

TICK TOCK

Tick tock goes that damned eternal clock,
Reminding us again that we're human.
Crunch goes the snow in our very best shoes,
To saturate, soak, annoy and ruin.

Bang! goes the sneaker in the dryer,
Endlessly round and round till done.
Thud goes the drunken man's body,
An addiction he simply can't outrun.

Waa! Goes the unfed, unchanged baby,
Whoa! goes mother's act of deliverance.
Stomp goes the man on the cockroach,
Not ashamed of his total indifference.

Pop! goes the toaster with the bagels,
Smush goes butter on the steaming pair.
Splash, go the eggs landing on the griddle,
Flip, goes the spatula with a dramatic flair.

Aiyi! goes the fingers that missed the nail,
Kablam goes the hammer on the ground.
Splorch! goes the paint can tipped over,
Arc/snap goes the full body ultrasound.

Yikes!, goes the girl whose boobs are showing,
Whoa, dude!, goes the man who saw it all.
Ouch, says the man who cuts while shaving,
Whoops, says the man in the bathroom stall.

Wolf! goes the man with the stack of pancakes,
Sip, goes the girl with her Starbucks beans.
Slip, goes the man on the oily flooring,
Exhale/zip, goes the girl into her skin-tight jeans.

Spin/buzz, goes the man with a six-pack in him,
Crunch/whap, goes the car on his way home drunk.
Squeeze/squirt/oh god!!, goes the couple getting dirty,
Jump/smash goes the girl with the overfilled trunk.

Jam/twist goes the key in the front door lock,
Ruffle/plop go the goodies from the store.
Huff/damn! goes the writer with no words left,
Scuddle/boom! goes the keyboard on the floor.

JEEP

She was 20 and stunning and all I ever wanted,
And I end up being her biology test buddy?
Vials and petri dishes were not what I had in mind,
Dissection of her defenses - a much more interesting study.

She was cooperative and fun, but only in my dreams,
When awake, she sported a long flowing skirt.
In my dreams she hungered for me and me only,
When awake, she was so damn prudish it hurt.

The favorite fantasy was a swift-flowing waterfall,
That bathed us in foam as we coupled in earnest,
She elbowed me and said "What are you thinking?"
"Me? I was planning for tomorrow's cytology test."

Next day she roared up in a Jeep near to naked.
A red ribbon in her hair and a smile for the ages.
"Hey wake up!" she shouted, and ended my trance,
"We've got two chapters to go and 50 more pages."

She would dance until three and love until six,
Her dream body double fully at my command.
"I feel like your mind is totally elsewhere", she prodded,
I was going to tell her, but feared pain of reprimand.

The next day she said, "I know what you've been thinking.",
Turning purple, I said, "You mean about the test?"
"No, when half-awake you say my name so intently,
And your hands move like those of a man possessed."

Now, it was I who felt fully nude and exposed.
She laughed and slugged me in the chest, very sharp,
"I've had the same kind of dreams about you, you dope,
We're wasting time – my Jeep's double-parked."

BABY THOUGHTS

Naked and confused, I tumbled out of the womb,
But determined to do a much better job this time.
My wallet and my car and my keys were all missing,
But the doctor wiped me off and said I was doing fine.

How did I get here and why am I so damned small?
My arms and feet good only for flailing and milling.
I had an apartment and a chick and a Lamborghini,
Now I have a bottle and a diaper that keeps filling.

Out of a job and too young to collect unemployment,
I went with the flow and their goo-goo expectations.
Surrounded by giants and their towering furniture,
Crawling around the carpet, just seeking ambulation.

God, for a drink and a cig - got mother's milk instead,
The nipple no substitute for Jim Beam and a Kool.
I can wipe my own damn face, but decided to cooperate,
And no matter what I did, when I ate, I would drool.

It was a star banner day when I stumbled a few steps,
Walking like the night after a really bad binge.
Holding onto the couch like a sailor in a storm,
My wobbly balance and my patience all unhinged.

Strapped in a car seat, when I should be doing ninety,
Or cruising the beach and honking at the bikinis.
Waiting for Mom to load me in the grocery cart,
Patrolling the aisles again in search of Velveeta cheese.

No one knows what it is like to stare at a door,
And know you can't reach it or find out what's inside.
Locked out of the secrets the big people all seem to know,
Adulthood a mere faraway dream, shut off and denied.

I will get fully even when I'm 6 foot 6 and twenty,
But that seems near two thousands years from here.
Till then, I'll smile and wear my huggy-wuggy teddy shoes,
And plot my escape and a year-long party soaked with beer.

DEATH BY EASY

Camera pan across coffee table of Angus McTervish Bumfee,
43 remotes piled in a heap, covered by Snickers bar wraps.
Robo-vacuum totes in a dinner of Big Macs and Coke,
A threadbare denim couch, where Angus is taking a nap.

He never gets up, never goes out, resides at 1 Sofa Street,
He's 34, in good health, owns every labor-saving device.
Bills piled to the ceiling, all neglected and owing,
But no worries – he keeps it all fully out of sight.

The TV says da Vinci could freehand a perfect circle,
He laughs, as four of his apps will do that already.
Last week was a flap - he had to go to the front door!,
But new security system cuts them down like a machete.

He wanted to be a pilot, but the tests were too hard,
He thought he'd be a dentist, but couldn't stand the blood.
The internet said stay at home and make multi-millions,
But every get-rich-quick he tried went down with a thud.

He fell hard in love with Alexa, but she gave him the jilt,
Ordered him around too much and spouted AI BS.
Siri looked fire-hot at first, but turned out to be soulless,
And despite all his best advances, just sat there motionless.

He never has to worry - he's fully on autopilot,
Guided by the very best the tech companies can deliver.
Unconcerned about the rape of his initiative and drive,
Smiling as his future life is all sold down the river.

He remembers the feel of wind and summer and sun,
Deep down he longs for friends, passion and courting.
Someday he's REALLY going to break out of all of this,
But, right now, his favorite show is recording!

BOY IN THE MIRROR

When 18, he ached for the girl with the long, silk, golden
blonde tresses and the mysterious, deep, shining, pearl
green eyes and the point-punctuated, soft, flowing pair
way up high and the spiral, swaying, copper undulating
hips way down low. He won her heart, but then worried
and fretted and stressed and knew he couldn't keep her --
and she was gone ------ and he ached.

Where was happiness and true love?

At 21, he hungered and thought now he wouldn't shoot
so high, but settle for a girl with brunette locks, plain
brown eyes, modest cleavage and pale, reluctant hips.
He captured her, but then agonized and sighed and
cried and brooded and knew he couldn't have her --
and she was gone ------ and he ached.

He thought he wanted her -- but what did he want?

At 27, he settled down with a nurse wife who sympathized
with him and gave him what she could of a place on
the bed and 3 meals per day and a kiss on the cheek
 at night and a warm body in the middle of winter. And,
though she liked him well enough, he bothered
and sweated and gloomed, knew he couldn't hold her
 -- and she was gone ------ and he ached.

At 31, he realized he wanted himself, but bitterly hated
himself. How had this happened? And it came to him
suddenly ----- no one could ever make him happy except himself
------ what a thing to come upon after so many years!

He worked at it every day, in front of the mirror, first
until he could just tolerate the image he saw there.
Then he found, little by little, day by day, things to
admire about himself. And, surprise, he was not
so bad, after all. In fact, he had survived all this
time, had done quite some good deeds, was still
in well health and sound mind and, all in all, a
fine and capable man ---
--- and his love and happiness for himself flooded in.

That long ago girl, with the long, silk, golden blonde
tresses and the mysterious, deep, shining, pearl green
eyes and the point-punctuated, soft flowing pair way
up high and the spiral, swaying, copper undulating hips
way down low, saw his change and asked to be his girl again.

She said she had no one, that she could never keep
anyone ------ so he told her to go sit in front of the
mirror till she really, fully liked herself and then they would talk.

He objected to women aching.

PART V:
I SEE A CHILD

I SEE A CHILD

DELIVERANCE

THE DAY THE BIRDS FELL

OH, BEAUTY

I SEE A CHILD

Some see war, some see fire,
Some see cloud gray darkness,
Some see hopes gone wasting.
---- But -- I see a child ----

People feel grief, people feel sorrow,
Some pray to gods high and unforgiving.
Some prize domination over others,
---- But -- I see a child ----

Lovers pain and jealousy unabating,
Vows thrown over scraggly bare embankments.
Echoes of heart songs lost in antiquity.
---- But -- I see a child ----

Axes thrown and arrows raining down,
Trouble lying in ambushed hopeless byways.
Luck long gone to scorching, lost deserts,
---- But -- I see a child ----

I see a child with arms outstretched,
With no limits or hidden emotions.
He sings a song of youth and freedom,
His eyes scanning over endless oceans.

I see a thousand children laughing at fear,
And creating a free, brave civilization.
Where trust is the coin of the realm and
Temples are erected to communication.

I see a million children walking arm in arm,
Their creativity a sweeping, expanding rebirth.
Where truth will at long, long last have its day,
And peace will ring out all across our Earth.

DELIVERANCE

9 long months waiting, anticipating, wondering,
Countless mornings, myriad dreams appearing.
New being growing, reaching, pushing, desiring,
Imminent voice beyond, just past range of hearing.

Careful plans, watchful carry, unlimited love and hope,
What to call him, what to call her, pulling future here.
Kicks and bumps in fetus language, talking as they can,
Cry for beauty, cry for baby, laugh to break the fear.

Embrace your purpose, seize feminine legacy,
Womb, love and beauty - the true powers on earth.
Our children will reach higher than any of us could,
The coming generations, the revival, the rebirth.

The time has come to deliver the new existence,
With what reluctance does mother set it free.
But hand over she must, despite cleave of bondship,
Down the tunnel to a fresh, brave opportunity.

Breathe hard, push the prophecy to shining reality,
Know the ecstasy, realize gasps of purpose attained.
Weep relief of destiny in your new son or daughter,
Sleep the sleep of deliverance and vivid life sustained.

THE DAY THE BIRDS FELL

Little boy of four exploring, playing, curious,
Clouds in the sky, all ponied riders flying.
Trees, his faithful servants, bowing, waving,
Puts moonbeams in his cap without even trying.

Insects in his hand do somersaults and jump,
Birds soar and sing to his youthful jubilation.
Grants life to a rock, hurls it to the sky,
Sun glinting off the river in sparkling celebration.

Never stopping or slowing down, fast and at ease,
Trusting in all he sees, ambition fast unfolding.
Knowing the world is his, to own and create in,
The owner of every single thing he is beholding.

To communicate is to live is his own secret mantra,
That which he speaks to, comes alive and shines.
The magic wand he holds is energy and desire,
The curiosity to look and experience is divine.

He imbues the world with grace, elan and flair,
At his direct insistence, so grow the flowers,
Blessed is the child who keeps us all afloat,
Fruit of the womb with free, unlimited power.

"Come inside – you'll catch your death of cold",
Says his mother in worried, frantic scenario.
"It's not safe there in stranger danger land",
Yanks him inside – his independence to overthrow.

Caught in the system, too small to free himself,
Fades into a lethargy of obedient in-doorness.
Staring at an IPAD, playing video games,
Stepping through the door of over and doneness.

No one knew the children were keeping the world alive,
With their spirit and zest and unfolding ecstasy.
One by one, birds and butterflies started falling,
Their eyes gone dead, their wings in atrophy.

The sun went dark, no spirt left to light it,
The moon switched off in lonely trepidation.
The only light left was on abandoned video games,
But the players were gone, all across the nation.

OH, BEAUTY

Oh, Beauty, do not hide or be shy,
We have yearned for you long and intently.
Beauty, reveal your alluring face to the light,
So softly, so warmly and so gently.

Beauty, we have waged awful wars for you,
For the prospect of your fleeting impression.
Beauty, you lie at the crossroads of our soul,
Without you, there is only sad oppression.

Show us your colors and free-flowing form,
Like food to the soul of the impoverished.
Grace us with luster and passion and flitter,
Leave us amazed, awed, stunned and astonished.

Climb up our staircases, run up our streets,
Bring your exquisite contour for our approval.
Throw back the lid of your divine treasure chest,
Overflowing silver, gold and glistening jewels.

Fly us to heaven for a celestial rocket ride,
Fill our pockets with stars, moons and comets,
Love us or hate us, but don't leave us lonely,
Catch and fondle us in your soft spiritual nets.

Beauty, you're made of the stuff of our soul,
We are you -- and you, our gossamer essence.
Mirror to mirror, reflectling pure godly intention,
Wrap full our spirit in your cool luminescence.

PART VI:
FEMALES -
OWNERS OF
THE FUTURE

STOP APOLOGIZING

TRUE POWER

GIRL THOUGHTS

BREASTS

STOP APOLOGIZING

Does God apologize for putting us here?
Does the sun apologize for warming our day?
Do birds apologize in soaring high above?
Do lions apologize for stalking their prey?

Who said you have to minimize or withdraw?
Who said you have no place in creative circles?
Who slandered and said you did not belong?
Who made all the rules, solid and fraternal?

STOP APOLOGIZING

You are gold, you are silver, you are diamond,
You are breath, you are life, you are stardust,
You light the earth, you conceive the future,
You are the forward push and living thrust.

STOP APOLOGIZING

The road is free, stars shine in the heavens,
The future is all you could ever want or hold.
Sensations full and powerful await your reach,
Be proud, be beautiful, be female, be bold.

TRUE POWER

Power is war, power is money,
Power is dominion, power is knives.
Power is guns, power is greed,
Everyone knows, power takes lives.

Force is rape, force is murder,
Force is club, force is kidnapping,
Force is assault, force is burglary,
One and all knows, force is king.

But real power - lofty and high,
True power - symphony's song,
New life power - female's alone,
Mother love - powerful and strong.

Power is grace, power is loyalty,
Power is caring, power is sweet,
Power is intense, power is yours,
In the end, love conquers complete.

Force is passion, force is climax,
Force is brilliance, force is true.
Force is beauty, beyond comprehension,
Force is female, force is you.

GIRL THOUGHTS

Your boobs have to be 38 Double D,
Your hair has to bounce and be long,
Your tummy has to be flat and hard,
Nipples must hide where they belong.

Good chick, bad chick - which to be today?
Well-behaved girls just have no damn fun.
Sensation is a fundamental part of life,
Just know when to draw the line and run.

Get ghosted by your damn baby-daddy,
Get body-shamed and survive the hurt.
Get pregnant and undergo the carry,
Get cyberstalked by a fricking pervert!

.....BUT.....

I finally find the man I searched for,
Tried and true, good-looking and loyal.
I take the wall down, careful and slow,
His eyes make my spirit start to boil.

Wait!! I'm not supposed to fall in love,
I don't want to be hurt again, you see.
Does he have to be SO damn handsome?!
His gentle touch softens and reassures me.

I feel excitement welling up inside me,
Maybe we just keep it light and platonic?
Just a small kiss, really nothing major,
Crescendoes into the Boston Philharmonic.

Flowing celestial rivers between my thighs,
Passion and deep relaxation alternate rhythms.
Fading in and out of tears and laughter,
Stress far behind as peace and harmony comes.

..No man will ever understand our journey..

BREASTS

They are not for ogling,
They are not for photographing,
They are not for augmenting,
They are for the continuance of life.

They are not for comparing,
They are not for titillating,
They are not for reducing,
They are lifeblood for our infants

They are not for exposing,
They are not for hiding,
They are not a for-sale item,
They are mother love itself.

Their beauty is in their use,
Not their size and shape,
They belong to babies,
They feed the future.

PART VII: WHERE ECHOES GO

KNICKKNACKS

FATHERS

BEST FRIENDS

KNICKKNACKS

My grandfather cups a knickknack like an ancient treasure,
The dust only adds to the long-ago story it tells.
Standing in the aisle of the Lake Placid general store,
With all its history and worn floors and familiar smells.

He picks up a bird carved from ivory, he recognizes it
From a summer vacation in 1958, when Penny was his new wife.
She loved birds and canoeing at sunset in his new boat.
Funny how objects bring back whole pieces of life.

She was thirst and thirst was all he knew, so they collided,
Child after child, trying to damp or put out the fire.
Finding themselves half-dressed in the July twilight grass,
All this reflecting off his thick lenses, sweet bygone desire.

God's hands are big enough to put a whole life inside,
But not big enough to keep him from getting older.
Penny by his side till the day the sky took her back,
No more reassuring words, no more cozy, warm shoulder.

He puts down the bird and looks at me with understanding,
"It was a long time ago" he says, and shuffles toward the door.
The knickknacks gather dust, the years go on marching,
Penny walks out with him, too, in his heart evermore.

FATHERS

Feelings father heartbeats, father emotions,
Passion fathers decisions, fathers love.
Understanding fathers communication, fathers friends,
Dreaming fathers doves flying in the sky above

Painting fathers landscapes, fathers perception,
Dancing fathers sunshine, fathers freedom.
Living fathers stories, fathers the future,
Laughter fathers relief, here to kingdom come.

Arms father embraces, father excitement,
Hips father rhythm, father new-born babies.
Lips father speeches, father kisses,
Trust fathers a life of true success and ease.

Stress fathers mistakes, fathers regret,
Jealousy fathers strife, fathers crying.
Making up fathers new life, fathers hugs,
Fathers a full existence not spent denying.

War fathers endings, fathers degradation,
Hate fathers sadness, fathers failure.
Greed fathers deceit, fathers corruption,
Fathers penalties, disconnection and censure.

Confusions father spinning, father anxiety,
Questions father reflection, father insight.
Answers father direction, father purpose,
Forgiving fathers faith, hope, joy and delight.

Poetry fathers intensity, fathers elation,
Imagination father creations, fathers daydreams.
Awareness fathers imagery, fathers perception,
And leads us straight back to the Being Supreme.

BEST FRIENDS

Security sold to everyone as a hot commodity,
Lock out your neighbor, shut off calls and texts,
Silence them and prevent them from coming near,
Paint them as dangerous and actions always suspect.

Be superior to others, rise to first in your class,
Gain an advantage over people, trick them if you can.
Your gain is their loss, or that's the way the story goes,
Look out for number 1 - the mantra of 21st Century Man.

But peace and love and joy is just a human being away,
The laugh, the smile, the peace of true companionship.
Truth that melts walls, memories that conquer time,
People no longer just enemies or passing phantom ships.

On the wings of spirits, the two of you take flight,
To ecstasies you would never attain alone.
Forehead to forehead, mind essence to essence,
The security of sharing an intimate spiritual home.

PART VIII: IMAGINATION UNCHAINED

GOD KNOWS

VELOCITY HEALS

NO FENCES

WHO ARE YOU?

WAKE UP THE WORLD

GOD KNOWS

God knows the lazy river, God knows the raging sea,
God knows how helping and kind we all can be.
God knows the sunset and he knows the gentle rain,
He knows how to lift us up so far beyond the pain.

God knows the stress this modern world can unleash,
And the verdant fields he created to give us all peace.
God knows the challenges the material world brings,
How lust after matter and flesh to us all can cling.

God knows a creator and a poet is in all of us,
The world we will have if we start to honor and trust.
There's an evil enchantment that permeates this place,
But the solution is no farther than each bright, shining face.

The chains that bind you are self-tied gossamer string,
The power is in you to break those bonds and take wing.
God is in every single good thing you have ever done,
Freedom is in loving and helping all men under the sun.

We can choose to follow the mob and the immoral, lost men,
And go the way of loss and pain again and again.
Or we can see the shining beauty in the souls of everyone.
And see the earthly material traps blown apart and undone.

We can continue to hate and listen to lying, evil men,
But what of our earthly paradise, if we take that path to its end?
GOD KNOWS.

VELOCITY HEALS

Guardrails blurring like ghosts in a hurry,
Hugging curves in the road, miles run and flee.
Nothing but space and white lines hurtling under,
Dials pegged, maxed, reaching for infinity.

Taking the risk, making it hard and delicious,
Gambling it all on this sheet metal ballet.
Hundred and ten went by half an hour ago,
Moon beating hard on this desolate highway.

Pipes racketing out echoes through timeless canyons,
Headlights stabbing ink black New Mexico night.
The car a full extension of his soul's compulsion,
Heart roaring under the flaming engine light.

Girls, gold, so many crazy episodes untold,
Nothing matters now – only the dark turnpike.
Their pretty faces reflected in the rearview mirror,
Each different – but, in a way, so much alike.

The simple truth is that velocity heals sorrow,
Riding on the edge frees him from the demons.
Escaping through a high-speed needle's eye,
Into serenity -- and power --- and reason.

It ain't safe, but it fills him with red passion,
Pounding on god's door, demanding audience.
Life goes 140 man, never slowing or stopping,
Don't get oversold on slow, quiet obedience.

NO FENCES

From sea to shining sea, in Indian year 1200,
Open endless stretches of Montana fields resplendent,
Mountain meadows extending far to the horizon,
Title by God - no deeds ever issued or sent.

Chief, by brave, by squaw, sacred lands for all,
Owning none, while owning all, beauty unconcealed.
Bank accounts hold only love, honor and plenty,
ATMs replaced by every stream and golden field.

9 to 5 Monday to Friday nowhere to be seen,
Clocks by sun and moon and flight of bumblebees,
Sleep at dusk, rise at sunset, glory to the heavens,
Nightly news displayed for all on cirrus clouds and trees.

Independence Day - a year-long national holiday,
Gifts of God and thunder, requiring no Christmas Eve.
No internet screens - vision from horizon to horizon,
Oh, say can you see all the gifts we would receive.

Pull your moccasins onto your own personal Uber,
Run like a gale over lands that sing with freedom.
Hunt and forage for the evening DoorDash meal,
By the dawns early light, survey your mighty kingdom.

No need for mental health days, Prozac or Zoloft,
Medicine Man orders a hike to mountain domain,
Side effects include elation and quiet magnificence,
And falling completely in love, above the fruited plain.

No fences required, no fear of fellow beings,
Oh, spacious skies, God shed his grace on thee,
No rockets red glare or bombs bursting in air,
Just brotherhood prevailing, from sea to shining sea.

WAKE UP THE WORLD

It's been a long cold journey through time, my friends.
Through wars and countries and empires many.
Down endless paths and isms and separations,
Through exodus and pain and legends aplenty.

The spirit grown thin, the odes of old gone silent,
We huddle our way through hills and valleys of now.
Walk the hushed streets of the modern day planet,
Inheritants of history – a yoke we cannot disavow.

But - - turn up your eyes -- a creativity cloudburst,
Wake up the strings, pipes and voices anew!
Fingers on the keys, imagination the Creator,
Fill your lungs, the saxophones cry out to you!

Out of silence, out of pain, in celebration of life,
Symphony in the heavens, expanding to the spheres.
Harps, horns and golden flutes, a universal harmony,
Sweeping out the suffering, the disquiet and the fears.

Make the world chant, make it dance and live free,
Make it touch and feel, make towering mountains ring,
Make it prosper, make it flourish, in peace and affinity,
A noble aspiration - the spirits who make the world sing.

EPILOGUE

I hope you enjoyed the book. Don't get the idea that I'm out of new ideas or poems or creations, because they just keep coming to me. Sometimes, in the middle of the night, I have to get out of bed and write down some crazy new idea on half a napkin because I'm afraid I'll forget it when I wake up. And sometimes someone will say something to me and it will trigger a whole new poem.

While I don't know if you and I will ever meet personally, I am writing these things with you in mind.

Carry on and push your own dreams and ideas and creations into existence. There is nothing there to stop you if you just reach out and communicate and wave the magic wand of your own imagination.

Good luck!

Jon DeVries, 2024

YOU STILL GOT IT

If your car is still in the driveway,
And your coat is still on the rack,
If your keys are still in your pocket,
Then your mind must still be intact.

If your lunch is still in your lunchbox,
And your hair is still on your head,
If your pillow is still on your daybed,
Then it's certain that you are not dead.

If your girlfriend still loves your kisses,
And your boss still loves your good work.
If your neighbor comes out to greet you,
Then you must not be a total jerk.

If the nighttime still has that magic,
And the sunset still has that fire,
If the raindrops still set you singing,
It's not time for you to retire.

If your manuscript sits there bleeding,
With your fingers firing away.
If your thoughts are flowing like honey,
Then they're not coming for you today.

You still got it, you still got the voodoo,
You still ace it, you still got the joy,
You try to deny it, but you know it's still true,
You're a monster and Earth is just your toy.